Intimacy With God

By

Patrick McIntyre

**WHITE
HARVEST
PUBLISHING**

Intimacy With God

Copyright 1992 by Patrick McIntyre
Published by White Harvest Publishing
Mammoth Spring, AR 72554

Library of Congress Catalog Card Number 92-91171
ISBN 0-9635050-0-9

Printed in the United States of America.

To the reader

You may find the best way to read Intimacy With God is one chapter a day. This way the truths of each chapter can be digested fully before continuing the book.

If you follow this suggestion, it will take a little over a month to read the entire book, and you will understand it more fully.

Thank you.

Patrick McIntyre

Table of Contents

Part 4: Understanding Your Choice

Part 5: Understanding Your Life

God Is The Reason For Living

When talking about God, you can make ultimate statements. For example, God doesn't just speak the truth, He is Truth. God doesn't just give love, He is Love. God doesn't just give us a reason for living, He is the reason for living.

Words can convey only so much. If you don't have a personal experience with the Living God, you'll never know He is the reason for living. Learning about Him is not the answer. What you should desire is to know Him as intimately as possible.

You can have a real relationship with the real God in your spirit. God can reveal Himself to you as you allow Him to speak to you. This is voluntary. The Holy Spirit is a gentleman. He will not force Himself on you. He wants you to ask Him deeper into your being. He wants you to invite Him to become your all in all.

This book can help you experience the Living God within you. It can help you live your life according to His perfect will, and allow you to experience His perfect love. Use it as a daily devotional and meditate on its biblical truths. You will feel joy in your life, and your personal happiness will increase as you attain an enriching, intimate relationship with the Holy Spirit.

The opinions in this book are based on biblical truth. But the Bible is truth itself. Do not be content with opinions. Read the truth of the Bible yourself.

Part One

Understanding
The Kingdom Of God

What Is Your Desire?

"Hope deferred makes the heart sick, but desire fulfilled is a tree of life." (Proverbs 13:12)

Desire is a good thing in itself. Without desire, you would not be human. Without desire, God would not be God.

Desire is the primary motive of life. Those who have no desire are dead, or may as well be.

Desire is neither moral nor immoral. Desire is amoral. If you desire a good thing, your desire is good. If you desire a bad thing, your desire is bad. God defines what is good and bad. If something is according to His will, it is good. If something is contrary to His will, it is bad.

If your desire is for God, then you don't have to worry much about what is good or bad, since He is the definition of good, and He will show you how to be like Himself.

If your desire is for God, your desire can be fulfilled. If your desire is for something other than God, your desire can be only partially fulfilled. You see, the things of God are the only things that will last. All the things you desire outside of God will perish with use, or be burned at the end of this age.

What does God want?

Many of us didn't have good parents. But those of us who did know that their desire was to help us grow to be like them, or even better.

They loved and encouraged us when we did something that showed we were becoming more like them. They loved us and disciplined us when we did something that showed we were becoming less like them.

With God it is the same way. He wants us to become just like Him. To become like God is to become all we were created to be. Deep down you know this is the reason you were born into this world: to become perfect in God, someday. In the Bible this is called the Blessed Hope.

To become perfect in God and to be One with God are the same thing. It is not a selfish thing. It is a union of God and man for the pleasure of both God and man. It is the reason for life. As

4

God is, so is the Blessed Hope.

If your desire is for God, you will draw nearer to Him no matter what the cost, and you will start to understand that the Blessed Hope is your reality. The Blessed Hope must become your desire. And your desire will be fulfilled.

The Still Small Voice

The Bible presents the voice of God in different ways. He is sometimes pictured as using the elements of His creation to reveal Himself to man.

"The Lord also thundered in the heavens, and the Most High uttered His voice, hailstones and coals of fire." (Psalm 18:13)

Man pictures God in the powerful forces of nature. Somehow we think that since God is all powerful, His voice must be very loud.

But to understand the power of God, don't think about atom bombs, earthquakes and lightning. Rather, think about the utter silence and seeming infinity of outer space.

Imagine yourself traveling away from the sun at one million

miles per hour without a sound. Do you "hear" the silence? Do you feel the endlessness? Do you see the trillions of stars all held in suspension by His hand? And even though you are traveling one million miles per hour, nothing seems to move.

Wonder at the unimaginable size of the universe. You could travel your whole life at incredible speed and never seem to get closer to the nearest point of light.

Now realize that God is bigger than this!

Go to the top of the highest mountain and look at the flowers no creature ever sees. Wonder at the inexpressible reality that God is there all the time. Now realize that a trillion miles away on an unknown planet there are things that no creature will ever look at nor even imagine, but God is there.

But God is bigger than this!

God is everywhere all at the same time. He is looking at every human being in the world. Not just down to the hairs on your head, but down to the movement of individual atoms and sub atoms.

The way that man sees the world is with selective eyes. He sees only what he thinks is important. He doesn't, for example, become concerned with his stomach unless it gives him pain. But God not only sees inside your stomach, He looks at what you're going to eat during the next ten years. In fact He knows what will be in your stomach when your body dies.

He knows what you're going to do at 9:16 a.m. on February 23, five years from now.

He knew you intimately even before you were conceived. Even before the foundation of the world. He knows your every pleasure and every hurt. He knows exactly why you are the way you are. He was there when you had your first nightmare. He felt your pain when you were told of a death in the family. He was there every step of the way as you learned little things about Him. He gave you small signs that assured you He was real.

He's known your every thought since your brain started to work. He talked to you in ways you would hear long before you invited Him into your spirit. He wooed you, and drew you unto Himself. He gave you the faith to accept Him as your Saviour and Lord.

And now He wants to talk to you all the time in a still small voice (1 Kings 19:12 KJV). He wants you to desire His words more than anything in the world, more than the desires of your heart and mind. But He will not override your distractions. He wants you to turn off the busy noise in your life so that you can give all your attention to Him.

He wants you to hear Him and speak to Him. He wants to have a continuous conversation with you. He wants you to be so aware of His presence that you'll make Him the center of all you think and do.

God's voice is like radio waves. You can't see them, and you can't hear them without a receiver tuned to the correct frequency. Your spirit needs to be tuned into God. Only then will you receive His transmission.

Those around you may be completely unaware that the Holy Spirit is there in great power. But you will know. And as you turn to him day by day, His still small voice will become clearer to you.

Intimacy In The Spirit

In old Israel, when a couple married, the law said that they were to spend a year together before any separation for war service.

Perhaps new Christians should take a year for intimacy with Jesus, their spiritual spouse, before going out onto the battlefield of religious service.

They need to have a personal revelation of God's love for them. They need to receive the nurturing and care of God. They need to develop an intimate two-way relationship based on trust and love. They need to understand grace as the love of God, not as an abstract "gift" given as an escape ticket to heaven.

Grace can be truly understood only in intimate relationship with Jesus.

Each person must come to know Jesus on his own. Each person must personally invite Him into his deepest being.

Unlike laws, rules, and traditions, a relationship with Jesus cannot be given to a group. Jesus must be experienced personally. Because it is so personal, this relationship cannot be passed down from father to son, or mother to daughter. The child can see the parents' commitment to an invisible God, but that doesn't mean that the child has received God personally.

The desire of God is that you have faith working through love. If you have faith in Him, He does the work. You experience His peace, joy and love as the result of walking in faith.

You are one spirit with God. As two people come together in marriage and they are made one flesh, so when God married Himself to you, you became one spirit with Him. This is by His choice. God is a perfect partner who is always there and who always does what's best for your relationship. He is never unfaithful. He loves you unconditionally.

If these words seem like pretty sentiments, and you have yet to experience intimacy with Him, then continue walking in faith. Praise God. Worship Him. Open yourself up to Him. Ask Him to reveal Himself to you. As you read this book, ask Him to teach you, in your mind and heart and spirit, so that you might be an intimate bride to Him.

In The Beginning

Adam and Eve knew God intimately. They lived on this earth like we do, but their life was not like our life. We came into the story of man after several chapters. We never experienced the LIFE that Adam and Eve knew with God before the fall.

God IS. He is THE primary existence. The name He gave Himself was "I AM that I Am." That is, "The Self Existent One."

God is the only one who should be selfish. For God to be

selfish is good for all His creation, since He is the definition of good. If God wants something, it is good. What makes it good is that God wants it, and it is good only because God wants it. As Jesus said, only God is good.

In the same way there is life only in God. He is the definition of life, and real life can come only from Him. All life outside of Him is not really life. It is merely existence.

Adam and Eve knew Him face to face. They knew Him as THE life. They didn't know about Him. They knew Him. To know about someone you have to make a comparison in your mind. You have to have some knowledge of good and evil. You have to make a judgement. Adam and Eve could do none of these things. In the state in which they were created, they had no ability to judge right from wrong, or good from bad. They also had no conscience or instinct.

In fact, none of the creatures on earth, before the fall, had instinct or conscience. This is why animals did not kill one another. It was only at the fall that the creatures received this instinct.

Created beings had no reason for self-motivation and self-preservation. They lived by the intuitive knowledge of what was good, from God. They lived as a baby in the womb lives by the life of its mother.

Adam and Eve were connected to God in their spirits. As long as they chose to live by this intimate relationship, they experienced the real life of God flowing into their beings, moment by moment.

Adam and Eve were given all the animals to rule over. This was God's pleasure. Adam and Eve were the king and queen of the kingdom of earth. When they walked with God, all the kingdom of earth walked with God. But when they chose to sever their life link with God, He withdrew His provision from them, and from all in their kingdom.

But God took pity and gave each creature its own internal

guide. This guide would enable it to survive without His direct help. He gave it instinct; to Adam and eve He also gave conscience.

When Adam and Eve ate of the Tree of the Knowledge of Good and Evil, God withdrew His life from them. His life stopped flowing to His creation.

Adam and Eve no longer listened to God in their spirits, and their spirits were dead to God. They heard two new voices to guide them: instinct and conscience.

The voice of instinct told them to look out for themselves. To be self-centered, not God-centered. To be self-conscious, not God-conscious. To serve self, not God.

The voice of conscience told them that they were guilty. They had done wrong, and they needed to pay for their offence to God. They were caught in a desperate struggle that persists to this day: knowing that their existence is wrong, and not being able to do anything about it.

Instead of seeing God as a loving Father, they now saw Him as the enemy of their selves. Loving God had been their reason for living. Now, pleasing self was their reason for existing. They were confused, as mankind is today, for they couldn't feel His love. When they knew His love, everything made sense. Now, all they had were carnal desires and a pile of ashes.

Before Adam and Eve ate from the Tree of the Knowledge of Good and Evil, they had no concept of sin. They knew only life -- God Himself. The only issue for them was obedience to God. As long as they obeyed God, sin was unknown.

When they lost fellowship with God, they stopped experiencing God's life. Now they experienced self life. A life of survival of the fittest. A life filled with fear, doubt and pain.

Two Trees To Choose From

Adam and Eve once lived by God's life. They were used to knowing God's will by intuitive knowledge in their spirits. They received it moment by moment. After they disobeyed they did not know God's will. They existed by a limited knowledge of good and evil.

Instead of receiving intuitive knowledge from God of what to do, they had to figure out what was best with their own knowledge of good and evil. It was a cheap substitute for the leading of the Holy Spirit.

Man became his own god. A lousy god, with little knowledge, and one who makes mistakes. God never makes mistakes because he is omniscient. Man's error is that he thinks he knows enough to be a good god. That's why Jesus said that only God is good.

But Adam and Eve had to survive, so they left the Garden of Eden and made an existence for themselves.

They knew the pain of separation from God, and knew the desolation of self. They found within them the seeds of all kinds of sin and corruption. God reached out to their descendants through prophets. Mankind learned from them how holy God is and how sinful man is, and how, without a Redeemer, there was no chance of them ever coming together.

God sent laws to help them understand their sin, and their knowledge of good and evil increased. But it didn't cure the sin. There was only one cure: the Tree of Life.

The prophets foretold of a time when man would once again enjoy intimacy with God, when God would renew the relationship broken so long ago. God was prepared to give man His life again.

First the sin of mankind would be paid for by God Himself, in the person of the Lord Jesus Christ. The name Jesus, in the original language, means Jehovah (God) saves. But when Jesus came, many didn't understand that they needed to be saved. The religious community, in particular, thought they were good because they possessed an extensive knowledge of good and evil.

They had eaten of the Tree of the Knowledge of Good and Evil to the point that they thought they had life. Jesus tried to tell them He was the Life. Jesus is the same life that Adam and Eve experienced: the Life of God. But the religious leaders chose their own knowledge of good and evil instead of God's life. They rejected their Redeemer.

Jesus came as the seed of The Tree of Life. They planted Him in the ground and He rose again as the Tree of Life. So that whoever would come to Him should not die, but have everlasting life (John 3:16), thus fulfilling the words of God in the Garden of Eden. They would eat of the fruit of the Tree of Life and live forever.

When you truly eat of the Tree of Life, you are born again. You experience the life of God. All things seem new. But after a while, many people start relying on themselves again. They resume eating from the Tree of the Knowledge of Good and Evil and reject the Tree of Life.

The fruit of the Tree of the Knowledge of Good and Evil is information and ideas. It appeals to your mind and heart. It says, "I'll help you protect yourself! Possess the knowledge of good and evil, and be your own judge. You are as God. You can be self-led!"

The fruit of the Tree of Life is real life from God, and it flows moment by moment. It brings with it all you need. It provides you with intuitive knowledge of God's will. You will be led by the Holy Spirit. So do not be content with your own self-existence. Eat of God's life and really live.

The choice of whether you eat of the Tree of the Knowledge of Good and Evil or the Tree of Life is a reality every moment of every day. It is the choice of whether you'll listen to what your heart and mind say, or to what Jesus says in your spirit.

New wine needs to be poured into a new wineskin. New cloth needs to be sewn onto a new garment. Jesus brought true Life. It can only be understood and experienced by a Spirit-led Christian. Let us partake of it continually.

"But now we have been released from the law, having died to that by which we were bound, so that we serve in newness of the Spirit and not in oldness of the letter." (Romans 7:6)

The Bible

The Bible is essential for a Spirit-led walk.

The Bible is the only foolproof authority concerning God's will for man. It gives you security in your walk with Jesus. Without it, you will lack confidence in the voice of the Holy Spirit. With it, you will be able to confirm that you truly are hearing from God.

The Bible will help you not to be fearful. Faith and love are greater than fear. You are a child of the living God and fear should not rule you in any way.

You should expect that sooner or later, your spiritual enemy, Satan, will speak to you in a voice that sounds something like the Holy Spirit. If you are reluctant to listen for the Holy Spirit's voice because you're afraid you'll hear from the enemy, trust that God is in control.

For example, a married woman who is afraid of childbirth might become frigid, even though her doctor reassures her any danger is minimal. It is part of life that threatening things exist, but we must not stop living for fear of them.

Even as the married woman overcomes her fear and welcomes her husband with love, so we Christians must mature and believe that we are the bride of Christ, and become more intimate with Him.

Safety rule #1

Do not listen to any voice that goes contrary to the Bible.

Safety rule #2

If the contrary voice persists, take counsel. Go to your pastor and talk to him in depth about it. If you act in pride, you can be sure you're not hearing from the Holy Spirit. Make no major decisions until you've received counsel.

Safety rule #3

Read your Bible day in and day out. Let it become a part of you. It is the only foolproof way of determining what is of God. Not only will it prevent you from falling into the enemy's snare, it will help you tell the difference between your soul (heart and mind) and your spirit.

"For the word of God is living and active and sharper than any two-edged sword, and piercing as far as the division of soul and spirit, of both joints and marrow, and able to judge the thoughts and intentions of the heart." (Hebrews 4:12)

As you read the Bible, the Holy Spirit will make certain passages come alive. You will learn quickly as the author of the Bible shows you what He wants you to know.

The Bible has all the answers to the basic questions of how to please God. You'll want to read the book He wrote to get to know Him better.

Also, use the Bible in prayer. Personalize the scripture as you speak to God. It is a way of inviting God to be more intimate with you. You might speak one of the Psalms to God the way David did originally.

The Bible says that David was a man after God's own heart. David enjoyed intimacy with God. Speak the Psalms to God as worship and you will sense His presence.

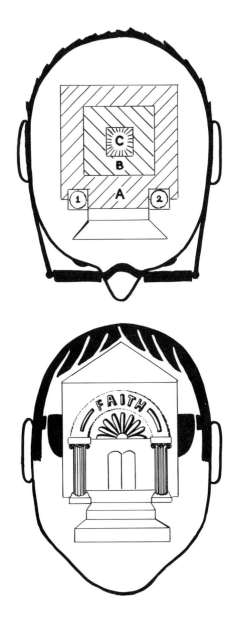

You Are The Temple Of The Holy Spirit

You were created to have fellowship with God. God put a place inside of you where He can live: your spirit.

Jesus said that up until His time there was none greater than John the Baptist, but that the least in the kingdom of heaven is greater than he. Up until John the Baptist, men could have an anointing of the Holy Spirit upon them, but not in them. Even Moses, David and Elijah did not experience the Holy Spirit within them.

Jesus promised that once He paid for our sins, He would send the Holy Spirit to live inside of us (John 14:16-17). This indwelling, which is the fulfillment of numerous Old Testament prophecies, is possible only after the spirit of each believer is cleansed by His blood.

The Greek word used in the Bible to say the Holy Spirit is *in* you is the same word used to describe Jesus being *in* Mary after she conceived.

It is commonly said the born-again Christian has Jesus in his heart. But it is scripturally correct that Jesus is in your spirit by the Holy Spirit.

This is more than a thought or concept. It is more than just a point of view, or merely a renewing of the mind. It is a spiritual fact. The Holy Spirit is in your spirit.

Once again it is possible for God to dwell in man, and it is possible for Christians, like Adam and Eve before the fall, to attain unbroken fellowship with God.

The Bible describes each born-again Christian as a sacred place of worship that shelters the Holy Spirit: "Or do you not know that your body is a temple of the Holy Spirit who is in you, whom you have from God, and that you are not your own? (1 Corinthians 6:19)

If you look at yourself as the temple of the Holy Spirit, you will see that many temple scriptures, as well as temple analogies, apply to yourself.

For example, you might view the temple's outer courtyard as your physical body. The inner court is your soul, or heart and mind (described in detail later). And the temple's Holy of Holies is your spirit.

The temple of a believer also has two pillars of faith: Jesus is your Savior, and Jesus is your Lord (see next two chapters).

What a responsibility you have! And what an incredible thing it is that the Creator of the Universe would dwell within you! This can be humbling, and even a bit puzzling, until you understand what it is that God wants to do in you.

Part Two

Understanding
Your Faith

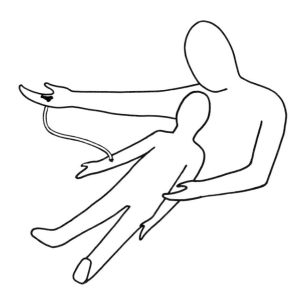

Pillar Of faith #1

Jesus is your Savior

The first pillar of faith is knowing that

GOD LOVES YOU AND ALWAYS WANTS WHAT'S BEST FOR YOU.

God loves you unconditionally. Regardless of how you feel, you must keep in mind that God loves you. He loves you not because of who you are, what you do, or who you might become.

God loves you because of who <u>He</u> is.

It is God's nature to love. In fact, GOD IS LOVE. Do not think you need to please God in order for Him to love you.

That kind of love is restricted by limited human understanding. God's love has nothing to do with our actions.

It bears repeating: Our faith must be anchored in the knowledge that God loves us because of who <u>He</u> is, not because of who <u>we</u> are, or anything we do.

If you make a mistake, God doesn't love you any less. If you sin, God doesn't love you any less. If you tell Him, "I hate you," He doesn't love you any less. He loves the worst sinner as much as the highest achiever in the kingdom of God.

God's love is His nature. God is love, and He cannot deny Himself.

If a friend turns on you and steals from you and makes fun of you and tries to destroy you, you would soon hate him -- unless you had the love of God in you.

Jesus exhorts us to "love your enemies, and pray for those who persecute you" (Matthew 5:44). Paul adds, "bless those who persecute you; bless and curse not" (Romans 12:14). As difficult as this seems, doing good to those who hate us can be a reality when we have the love of God within us.

Jesus Gave It All

When life beats us down we naturally feel unlovable. But Christ suffered and died for us so that we might feel loved. His blood is our life source, the love of God in action.

Even though He knows you well, He loves you unconditionally. He wants to change you by His power, but this is not a condition of His love. If you sin, you may walk away from His presence and not feel His love, but he continues to love you just the same.

Unconditional love should go both ways

We know from the Bible that God has unconditional love for us. God's goal is that we have unconditional love for Him.

Unconditional love should go both ways. When you experience hard times, He is still worthy of your love. And that brings us to the second pillar of faith.

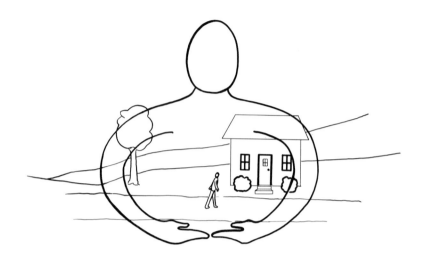

Pillar Of faith #2

Jesus is your Lord

The second pillar of faith is knowing that

EVERYTHING THAT HAPPENS TO YOU IS EITHER CAUSED BY OR ALLOWED BY GOD.

This sort of faith is easy to have when things are going your way. But it is hard when things aren't to your liking.

With this faith you learn that your perception of what is best for you is shortsighted. You come to rely on God for the definition of what is best for you.

All the great spiritual giants of the Bible had to endure suffering as a part of their maturing process. It is the way that God develops character in you. But rather than seeing this as a punishment or becoming fearful, view it as an opportunity to increase your faith and to more fully experience the love of God.

God may give a person wonderful talents, but the person may lack character. Character is not a gift of God, it is a virtue you attain through effort, over a period of time. And you are not powerless during the process. You can determine how long and painful each trial will be. If you submit to God quickly, you may suffer only bruises. If you resist God, you can make it much harder on yourself.

Change happens from the inside out, but it doesn't happen by forcing yourself to become something you're not. It comes by cooperating with the Holy Spirit as He shows you what to do.

The faith to do this comes only by truly believing that you are in the palm of God's hand at all times. Nothing happens that God doesn't cause or allow. He sees everything and may allow anything while you are walking with Him.

If you walk away from Him, He will allow things (which may appear to you to be bad or good) to happen that will bring you back to Him. He does this because He always wants what's best for you. He IS what's best for you. God IS the definition of good. As you draw closer to Him, you'll experience Good in it's eternal form.

Ask God to help you learn to love Him unconditionally. As you learn this unconditional love, you will grow quickly in the Spirit.

Faith And Testing

Let's say that your car is stolen. What do you say to Jesus? Perhaps you might say, "You blew it!" This response is obviously wrong. No Christian believes God makes mistakes.

Or perhaps you might say, "The devil did this." This response is also incorrect, for in itself, it doesn't address the true faith issue. Who's responsible for what happens in your life, God or Satan? Satan does only what God allows. So the correct response to the testing cannot be simply, "The devil did this." If we are to mature in our relationship with Jesus, we must understand without any doubt that He is Lord of everything in our lives.

When the waves were crashing over their boat and the disciples called out in fear for their lives, Jesus said to them,

"Where is your faith?" (Luke 8:24-25) Jesus was dismayed that the disciples would lose faith in God's care merely because of a testing.

The Faith Dynamic

When you judge a circumstance -- such as your car being stolen -- with your limited human understanding, you may see it as a calamity. Your faith in God's protection is likely to receive a serious blow. But if you say to Jesus, "I know you allowed this for a purpose, and I trust you. Thank you for working in my life," your faith in God will increase.

In fact, the more you suffer in the acknowledged will of God, the greater your faith will become. This bears repeating: You <u>must</u> understand that suffering is the result of God's allowing the circumstance to happen to you, and you must receive it with the correct attitude in order to grow in faith.

This is the Faith Dynamic. Nothing can increase your faith in God faster or greater than enduring pain knowingly for Jesus' sake. This does not mean we should desire to have pain so that we can increase in faith. Rather, we should recognize that we must go though testing, and bear it correctly, in order to increase our faith.

It needs to be said at this point that there is no virtue in hypocrisy. If you cannot say with love to Jesus, "You allowed this for a purpose, and I trust you. Thank you for working in my life," then don't say it at all.

This is a difficult concept. We'll discuss, in later chapters, how you can practice this love and perfect your response to the will of God in your life.

God Is Always There

Wherever you go and whatever you do, God is there. If you were to go to the bottom of the ocean or take a space ship to the moon, God would be with you. When you walk in the Spirit, this becomes reality to you. Even if you should lose a finger in an auto accident, God would be right there with you, loving you.

Some Christians grow in "faith" as long as everything goes their way. But when things seem to go wrong, they lose faith in God by saying in their hearts that God didn't have anything to do with it. Which means that God doesn't have anything to do with a lot of things in their life. It also means that God is really not the Lord of their entire lives, but of only a portion.

The meaning of Jehovah Jirah

All Christians say they "trust in God." What many mean by this is that they trust that God will take care of their needs and some of their wants. They look at God as "Jehovah Jirah," which modern theologians translate as "The Lord Provider." This perception of God works for people most of the time, but when a car is stolen, they are dazed and confused. They reel in instability, for their "faith" in God has been proved, it seems, to be too high. They slap themselves in the face and say, "Grow up! God isn't here to wipe your nose every time you sniffle." Their "faith" in Jehovah Jirah goes down a couple of notches.

Later on in their lives they may lose a finger in an auto accident, and their "faith" in God really takes a tumble. They may end up eventually on the trash heap of Christianity, blaming their separation from God on the devil's evil work.

But what if "Jehovah Jirah" doesn't mean "The Lord Provider"? The Hebrew words reveal a more profound meaning. The literal translation is "The Lord Who Sees." In the context of how it is used, it means, "The Lord Who Sees What We Need and Gives It." This is vastly different than a Santa Claus "Lord Provider."

"The Lord Who Sees What We Need And Gives It" is a true shepherd who knows what's best for His sheep, and who does what's best for them when they need it. It is similar to the New Testament concept of "bishop" or "episcopos," which means "overseer" or "shepherd."

A good shepherd will do what is best for His sheep. In some cases, this means breaking the leg of a rebellious lamb, in order to prevent it from wandering off and getting killed by wolves.

We must have faith that God loves us and always wants what's best for us, and we must have faith that everything that happens to us is either caused by or allowed by God. This faith is essential to our ability to give our lives fully to God, and to walk in the Spirit.

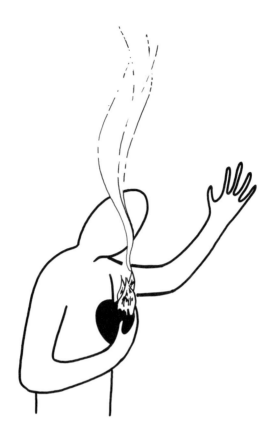

How To Die Gracefully

The apostle Paul spoke of being crucified with Christ: "it is no longer I who live, but Christ lives in me" (Galatians 2:20). Paul meant that he wanted to suffer the death of self so that Jesus could live through him.

But if you want to die to yourself, it is essential that you do it by the grace of God.

Without the grace of God, you'll accomplish nothing by suffering. If your attempt at self death is not by the permission and power of God, it is hypocrisy.

In his discourse on love, Paul said that even if he were to sacrifice his body and be burned alive, the act would be worthless without the leading of the love of God (1 Corinthians 13:3). And Jesus said that God desires mercy rather than sacrifice. (Matthew 9:13, 12:7).

If your dying to self is an attempt to prove something to God, don't do it. Jesus bought with His blood your entrance into God's presence. You don't need to sacrifice to persuade God to love you more. You sacrifice as you are led by God in order to mature in Him -- not to buy His love.

God will bring you through unpleasant experiences to purify you. If you know the grace of God is there as you go through these trials, then you can die to self gracefully -- full of God's grace.

When we die to self, our sacrifice becomes a voluntary cooperation with the Holy Spirit. Paul gave his body as a living and holy sacrifice to God, and he said we all should do the same. This consuming of self is a living sacrifice.

"I urge you therefore, brethren, by the mercies of God, to present your bodies a living and holy sacrifice, acceptable to God, which is your spiritual service of worship." (Romans 12:1)

Your life needs to be willingly offered to God. You need to willingly place your heart in God's hands, so that your heart can willingly be consumed by trials and tribulations. Let your heart continually be purified, continually lightened of self so that more of Jesus can live within you.

Pride, impure motives and carnal desires can be burned in the fire of the love of God. This burning of self comes by walking in faith through adversity.

As your heart is consumed by the fire of God's love, as with an Old Testament offering, the resulting aroma ascends to God as a pleasing sacrifice of love.

Sacrifice should never be done outside of the leading of God, nor outside His grace. It should always be done within His gentle leading. Learn to die gracefully, full of the grace of God, and you will soon see it as a friend to your relationship with Jesus Christ.

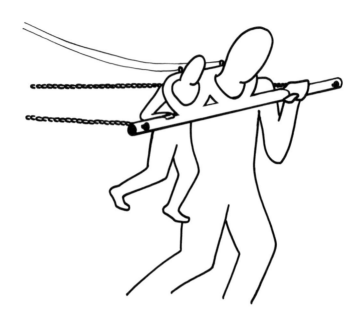

The Yoke Of Faith

You are yoked together with Jesus. He is in you and with you through the power of the Holy Spirit. His purpose is to live His life in you and through you so that you might know His life completely.

The way you are yoked together with Jesus is through faith, and the yoke of the Spirit is faith. The yoke is a wonderful thing that is necessary for your walk in the Spirit.

Many have tried to walk with God by walking beside Him, or by coming close to Him, but few actually wear His yoke of faith.

When you were born again you put on the yoke of faith. Wearing it is the only way a Christian can walk closely with God.

The yoke is wonderful and necessary for a Spirit-led walk. But without faith, the yoke pulls and binds, since the believer tends to go in a different direction than the Holy Spirit. The more you walk by your own strength, the more the yoke becomes a burden rather than a joy.

When you lose faith and forget about the yoke, life becomes difficult. If you continue in rebellion, you may even pull out of the yoke completely, thus losing your connection with the Holy Spirit. Then you are walking entirely by your own strength.

What an amazing thing it is, that the Creator of the universe would choose to be yoked with you -- and that He suffers when you forget the yoke of faith and try to walk by your own strength.

A lesson from the ox

When you observe animals in a yoke, you see two types. The first knows the yoke, and feels comfortable with it. It has no difficulty doing its work, because it allows the yokefellow to carry part of the burden. They walk in harmony, enjoying constant companionship and sharing, never trying to go different ways. They know how to wear the yoke, and it gives them comfort and security.

The second will fight the yoke and try to get out of it. It doesn't understand the importance of the yoke and how it can be a pleasure. It won't walk in harmony with its yokefellow, and is uncomfortable and unhappy. Its every desire is to escape what it sees as the work that the yoke brings. Because it is constantly resisting, it gets frustrated easily and tires quickly. Moreover, the work gets done slowly because it is continually interrupted as the rebellious animal tries to escape. And if the animal escapes from the yoke too many times, it is finally destroyed.

The Christian yoke

There is work to be done with Jesus, but His yoke is easy and His burden light (Matthew 12:30). This is possible because Jesus is your yokefellow by the power of the Holy Spirit. He does the work as you walk with Him in obedience. The yoke that binds you together is your faith. This faith is your belief that God loves you and always wants what's best for you -- as well as your knowledge that everything that happens to you is either caused by or allowed by God.

Two parts of the yoke are comforts the born-again Christian can depend upon: the neck pad and the guide strings.

The neck pad

This is a thick cushion of love that makes the yoke easy to bear. **It is experienced through your faith that God loves you and always wants what's best for you.** You know Jesus, as your Saviour, loved you so much that He died for you. The neck pad of faith is love from God Himself shed in your heart. Push against the pad. Bear down on it. Recognize it for what it is: a comfort purchased for you that you might live.

There is no burden so great that you cannot push against the pad and find comfort. Rely on it. Know that Jesus is your Saviour, Jesus is your Love. Remember that the pad is your faith in God's love for you, and that no matter what happens, you must continue to trust in His love. Push against it, bear down on it, pull your burden with the yoke of faith -- and you will feel the pad of love cushioning your shoulders.

The guide strings

The second comfort of the yoke of faith are the guide strings. These are held by the hand of God. Jesus is your Lord, and the guide strings are God's lordship over you. **They are experienced through your faith that everything that happens to you is either caused by or allowed by God.**

"All discipline for the moment seems not to be joyful, but sorrowful; yet to those who have been trained by it, afterwards it yields the peaceful fruit of righteousness." (Hebrews 12:11)

The Word Can Give Life

Jesus chided the religious rulers of His day for looking only to the scriptures for salvation when the living Word stood before them. Even today, some ignore the importance of the living Jesus and turn exclusively to the Bible for guidance. Others actually hurt people with the Bible. They don't understand that the law was created to bring man to God, not to separate him from God.

Jesus said to search the scripture, for it speaks of Him; He is the Light of the world. If you follow Him, you won't stumble through the darkness, for His living light will flood your path.

But some want to live by the Book without asking its Author to make it come alive for them. This is spiritual adultery. It is as if a man courted a woman and cherished her letters. Now, after they are married, he sits in the corner ignoring his wife while he reads her letters.

Many claim that the Bible is a lamp unto their feet and a light unto their path. This is true -- providing they have the help of the Holy Spirit.

False religions have resulted from people reading the Bible without the illumination of the Holy Spirit. A false religion may contain an element of truth, but it also will lure people away from a personal walk with Jesus.

Let's look to Jesus as our life. Read the Bible with Him and He will use the scriptures to lead you from glory to glory.

Part Three

Understanding
Your Self

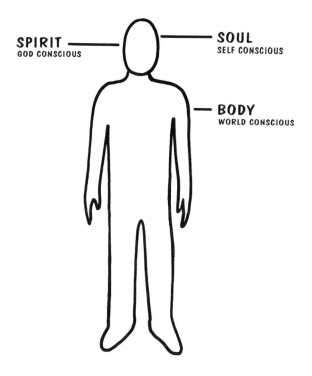

SPIRIT ———
GOD CONSCIOUS

——— SOUL
SELF CONSCIOUS

—— BODY
WORLD CONSCIOUS

You Are Three-In-One

You have three parts. God created you with a body, a soul and a spirit.

Your body

Your body is the easiest of the three to understand. It's the physical You that sees, hears, touches, smells and tastes. Your body is a shell for the other two parts.

Your soul

Your soul is composed of your mind, which thinks; your

heart, which feels; and your will, which chooses what's best for you.

Your spirit

Your spirit is where, if you are a born-again Christian, the Holy Spirit resides as a guest. Because of this, your spirit is a very important part of your being.

How they work together

These three parts work together as a team. For example, let's say you are walking down the street and your stomach grumbles. You know your body is saying, "It's time to eat." So your soul (your mind, heart and will) takes charge and tells the body to walk over to the hot dog stand. Your mind considers buying a hot dog, but then you hear from your spirit, "Don't you remember there's a special dinner waiting for you at home?" So you act according to the leading of the Holy Spirit and get on the bus for home.

All three parts of you were involved.

Your Mind, Heart And Spirit

You probably view the way you make decisions as a battle between your mind and heart. Each tries to win your will with persuasive arguments.

Your mind speaks to your will in objective terms. That is, with cold, hard, analytical thoughts.

Your heart speaks to your will with the subjective language of feelings and emotions.

But for a born-again Christian, there is a third voice that should be heard: the voice of the Holy Spirit speaking from within the spirit.

As we discussed earlier, the Holy Spirit speaks with a still, small voice. You cannot hear Him unless you turn all your attention to Him. He is always there even if you are unaware of His presence. If you want to walk in the Spirit, you must learn to hear His voice.

The language of the mind is objective thoughts.

The language of the heart is subjective feelings.

The language of the Spirit is intuitive knowledge.

The Holy Spirit speaks in a voice that comes as a sense of knowing. It is not facts and figures, but a complete idea that you somehow know is truth. It doesn't need to be figured out, it just IS. You accept it or reject it, but you can't rationalize it into something it is not. You either receive it as it comes, or you don't receive it at all.

The communication of the Holy Spirit comes straight from God. God knows everything. He doesn't have to figure things out like we do. He doesn't just possess knowledge, He IS knowledge. When God tells you something in your spirit, you know it is true.

This is why the language of the spirit is intuitive.

The way you can tell the difference between the voice of the Spirit and the voices of your mind and heart is that when you hear it, you know, deep within your being, that it is true.

For example, you wonder if you should buy a particular house. Your heart says, "Yes, it fulfills all my needs and desires."

Your mind says, "Are you crazy? It's a dump that will take years to fix up!"

In your spirit the Holy Spirit says only one thing. "Yes." That's all, just "Yes."

You ask your friends for advice, look at all the facts and say to God, "If I should buy this house, please make it very clear to me."

Over a period of time, God may show you specific reasons why it is a good thing to buy the house. In any case, it is your choice. If you don't buy it, God won't love you any less. He wants what's best for you. He knows you intimately and understands how you make decisions.

The Holy Spirit can change your plans, moment by moment. You may, for example, want to take revenge on someone by being mean to him, and the Holy Spirit will say, "Forgive him."

Or you'll want to do something that at first seems fun and the Holy Spirit will say, "That's not fun to me. Please stay with me."

Or you may feel lonely and left out, and the Holy Spirit will say, "I am here with you and I love you. Draw closer to Me."

As you learn what the voice of the Holy Spirit sounds like, you will be able to distinguish His voice from the voices of your mind and heart.

A word of caution: Even Spirit-led Christians sometimes misunderstand the Holy Spirit. There are no perfect walks in this life. Only Jesus walked perfectly in the Spirit.

Programmed For Success Or Failure

God created you with two more voices in your head: instinct and conscience.

Instinct

Instinct is like a computer program inside of you that works automatically to help you survive.

We are descended from Adam and Eve, who after the fall were given basic survival instincts. For those of us who don't have a strong will to live, instinct is what keeps us going.

Instincts are neither moral nor immoral; they are amoral. How you use them determines actions that are either moral or immoral. Moral is anything that is according to God's will. Immoral is anything not according to God's will.

It is amazing how many of our day-to-day thoughts and feelings are influenced by instinct. Pride, lust and greed are a few of them. Yet these same instincts stimulate self satisfaction, sexual desire within marriage, and the drive to provide for a family.

Instinct, because it is concerned with survival, gives a feeling of urgency and compels you to respond. It is the most "fleshly" of the voices in your head. Its "feeling" seems so much a part of you that it can be difficult to resist.

Example: You see a person who is sexually attractive to you -- even though your spouse is present. The attraction is triggered by the natural urge to procreate, which is amoral. Your conscience tells you that to act on your urge would be wrong. You mind, heart and will agree with your conscience and override your instinct, yet the attraction still exists.

A second example: A neighborhood boy throws a rock through your window. Your instinct tells you to protect your property. You feel compelled to go after the boy and punish him. The actual feeling within you is that you should kill him. Your conscience tells you that to do so would be wrong, and that you are overreacting. Yet the urge for retaliation feels right.

A third example: You come home from work hungry. You see a cake sitting on the counter. Your instinct tells you to eat it. Your conscience tells you to wait for dinner, and you do so, but your desire for the cake persists.

Conscience

Conscience is a person's best internal moral guide until he is born again. It is there to make you feel remorse when you do something you know is wrong. Also, more importantly, when God shows you something is wrong, your conscience reminds you of it.

The voice of instinct has urgency. The voice of conscience is calm, like a wise and caring parent.

Yet this parental voice has only as much wisdom as you and God give it. For example, if you believe a schoolmate when he says, "Step on a crack and break your mother's back," you'll feel guilt if you step on a crack.

Fortunately, you are born again and the Bible and the Holy Spirit are your guides. So now, if your conscience chides you for some irrelevant action, you have an advocate with God that is greater than that imperfect inner voice.

Nevertheless, God put conscience in you as a schoolmaster to lead you to Him. It works very well with the laws of God. It also speaks with a voice similar to the Spirit's.

As the Bible and the Holy Spirit transform your conscience with truth, your conscience will be a good friend. Having a clear conscience that doesn't condemn is essential in the Spirit-led walk. Many Christians never hear from the Holy Spirit because they are too busy dealing with their consciences. If your conscience bothers you, you must learn to deal with it correctly in the Holy Spirit.

When your conscience points out a sin, confess the sin to God. Ask God to tell you how to make it right. Then your conscience will no longer condemn you and cause guilt that will prevent you from hearing the Holy Spirit. Aim for "love from a pure heart and a good conscience and a sincere faith" (1 Timothy 1:5).

The Spirit-led Christian does not attempt to hide anything from God. All his flaws are visible. He allows his conscience to point out his faults continually. He then turns to the Bible and to the Holy Spirit for guidance on how to deal with his sins.

The sooner you deal with sin correctly, the easier it will become to recognize it and deal with it. A Spirit-led Christian can become so open that he sees sin instantly and deals with it immediately.

Unfortunately, many people fight with consciences that are always nagging at them. The Spirit-led Christian must get past the point of battling his conscience, and, with the help of the Holy Spirit, learn to use it as an excellent tool.

Final authority

The born-again Christian should understand that conscience is not the final authority; the Bible is. This truth is especially helpful when you are dealing with people caught in false religions. After all, a person's conscience can give back only knowledge it has received. So if a person has been taught that talking to people outside his particular cult is wrong, then he will feel guilty talking to you. His misinformed conscience will make him feel guilty.

The born-again Christian also must understand that his conscience is not the final authority over his own life. Jesus told us never to make a vow (Matthew 5:34). Making a vow is in the realm of trying to be God. The same principle is in effect when Christians make commitments to do that which is not in the will of God. Later, when God directs them to do something else, they suffer the guilt of conscience.

Remember Jephthah, who vowed to God that if he won a battle he would offer as a burnt sacrifice the first thing to come out of his house? (Judges 11: 29-40) He was horrified when his precious daughter became the sacrifice. Such things happen when we try to be God.

If the man had listened to the intent of the law, instead of the letter of the law, he would have spared his child. Jephthah's conscience told him he had to sacrifice his daughter. If he had read the scriptures and earnestly sought God on the matter, he surely would have seen that it was not God's will to make such a sacrifice -- and his conscience would have been satisfied with the light of God's truth.

CONSCIOUS MIND AND HEART

YOUR WILL CHOOSES WHOM YOU FELLOWSHIP WITH

UNCONSCIOUS MIND AND HEART

SPIRIT- WITH HOLY SPIRIT THERE

The Key To Happiness

We are told to rejoice in the Lord always (Philippians 4:4). But there are things inside of us that bring us down, things we don't understand.

Your soul (mind and heart) is the part of you that decides who you are and what you'll be. It is where you receive sensory information from your body. It contains your imagination, intelligence, emotion and most importantly, your will.

Before you were born again, you relied on your mind and heart for guidance and instruction. When you began to turn to the Bible and to the Holy Spirit, your mind and heart became adversaries that tried to pull you back to old ways of thinking and living.

You had become used to their rule over you, a rule you believed to be benevolent and trustworthy. In a way, they were your god.

It is not natural for man to trust God to carry his burdens. He naturally wants to be in control of all aspects of his life. It takes faith to believe that you can give your burdens to the Lord.

But now you are a new creature (2 Corinthians 5:17). You are no longer self-centered, but Christ-centered.

That old you is programmed with misinformation and faulty premises. Your mind and heart grew up in a sick environment, in a world run by a fallen race that has little knowledge of God.

As a born-again Christian, your job is to give all your attention to God. This is what it means to deny yourself (Matthew 16:24), and this is what is necessary in order to be Spirit-led.

Your mind and heart are where most of your troubles begin and end. Even though you received the Holy Spirit into your spirit and became a new creature in Christ, the old you is still there, contained in your memory, instinct and conscience.

These three are essential for the non-Christian, and for born-again Christians who do not walk in the Spirit. But those who walk in the Spirit follow a new way.

Spirit-led Christians judge and evaluate what their minds and hearts have to say before they take action. If your soul tells you something contrary to the Bible and the Holy Spirit, believe the Bible and the Holy Spirit and act accordingly.

This is the key to happiness: Believe that what God says is more important than what your mind and heart say, and allow yourself to be led by the Spirit. Do this continually, as an act of faith, and you will "rejoice in the Lord always."

A. Abandon Your Self

B. Believe in God

C. Confess Continually

The A B C Thing

Over a period of time, a born-again Christian will experience things he doesn't deal with properly in the Holy Spirit. These cause him to lose faith and fellowship with the Holy Spirit. (See: When a Dart Hits a Self-led Christian.)

Soon his unconscious mind and heart are cluttered with fears, doubts and confusion.

When he tries to rest in the Spirit, he finds only a discomfort he doesn't understand. This must be dealt with in the Spirit before fellowship with God can be renewed. It is why regular breaking (surrendering self to spirit) is necessary.

If you do not deal with things properly in the Spirit as they happen, you will have to deal with them eventually. The longer you continue in rebellion, the more difficult it will be to discern what's wrong within.

If you don't sense the presence of God, and you want the intimacy of His peace, joy and love, practice "the A B C thing": abandonment of self, belief in God, and confession of the truth.

Close the door and get alone with God. Kneel before Him and worship Him. Thank Him for all He does for you -- and more importantly, all He IS to you.

Ask His forgiveness for any wrong thing in you. Ask Him to reveal to you anything that stands between Him and you.

Expect Him to show you something or someone to pray for. Act as a yielded servant of the Holy Spirit. Give yourself to the service of God.

If you continue to feel confused, throw all your confusion into a box. Hand the box to God and say, "I don't know how I got this in me, but only You can sort it out. Please take it and let me experience Your life."

God will take away your confusion and flood your soul with His peace, joy, and love.

Do the A B C thing whenever you don't sense the presence of God, whenever you feel the need. It is similar to being born again. It will bring your relationship with God back to the basics.

You will have a clean slate to experience His life in the newness of the Spirit. You will once again experience what it is to be a new creature in Christ.

Confess Continually

Talk to Jesus about everything you do. Confess continually that He is your Lord and Saviour (Philippians 2:9-11).

Ask Him for what you need with thanksgiving, and ask Him for guidance even in small decisions. He wants to be your all in all.

Commune with Him continually, "and the peace of God, which surpasses all comprehension, shall guard your hearts and minds in Christ Jesus" (Philippians 4:7).

Pray at all times in the Spirit. Tell God how wonderful He is. Say to Him, "Thank you Jesus, Praise you Jesus. You are so wonderful. You love me even though I'm nothing," and so on.

"Rejoice in the Lord always, again I will say rejoice!" says Paul in Philippians 4:4. "Let your forbearing spirit be known to all men."

And in 1 Thessalonians 5: 16-19: "Rejoice always; pray without ceasing; in everything give thanks; for this is God's will for you in Christ Jesus. Do not quench the Spirit..."

So, build yourself up on your most holy faith, praying in the Holy Spirit.

And as you spend your entire day in communication with the Holy Spirit, you will grow spiritually. One day spent in close communication with the Spirit will cause you to grow more than three weeks of any other activity. Your spirit will become strong and you will become accustomed to hearing His voice.

When you walk in the Spirit, you have an unveiled face towards God. This transforms you from glory to glory. You will know Him in a more real way. He will help you with all the tasks of the day. It will be pleasant to have Him as your friend and companion in everything you do.

When you walk in the Spirit, it is almost impossible for an arrow of the enemy to reach you. Your continual confession to God is what occupies your mind. How can evil thoughts intrude when you're having a good time with Jesus? Think and speak the truth in love and you will be protected from mind pollution. You will align yourself with the reality which exists in the heavenlies.

Thoughts of how great God is are more than affirmations of faith. They are foundational truths to be repeated by us for eternity. Even after we no longer think with brains as we know them, we will continue to express these truths. These are eternal truths, primary truths, truths that never change.

You were not made to have to carry the burden of worrying about every little thing that could possibly happen. You've become used to protecting yourself by constantly thinking things over and over, but this is not good for the born-again Christian.

We are called to find out what God wants us to think, and then to think those thoughts.

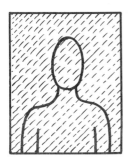 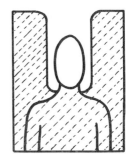

The self-led Christian is self-contained. He's led by systems of doctrine and morality evaluated by his mind. He relies on his knowledge of good and evil, trusts his soul (mind and heart) to lead him, and doesn't seek the leading of the Holy Spirit.

The Spirit-led Christian walks by the leading of the Holy Spirit. He has his own opinions, but values the Holy Spirit's intuitive leadings far more. He lives moment by moment in the living God.

Walking Moment By Moment

The Spirit-led Christian defines pleasure as knowing the life of God moment by moment. Feeling good means knowing that he is loved by God and that God is in control. The Spirit-led Christian enjoys feeling God's presence and His love. He desires nothing that displeases Jesus. He sees all things that happen to him as part of God's plan. And with that knowledge, he is able to endure all things. His whole life becomes a practice of faith working in love.

Before he was born again, he spent his life finding out things that "work" in the physical realm. He tried to protect himself from getting hurt, learned how to judge situations and circumstances with his limited knowledge of good and evil, and gathered as many facts as he could in order to reason, rationalize and protect himself.

He walked in his own knowledge, and he was his own god. He thought he had everything under control, and that his knowledge of good and evil would save him.

Then he became born again by accepting what God said instead of what his mind and heart said. The power to be born again came by faith in God to the exclusion of self.

Now he walks in the Spirit by faith in God, also to the exclusion of self. When he steps out in faith, rather than walking in his own knowledge of good and evil, he is walking in knowledge given by God moment by moment. He once lived by the leading of his own mind; now he lives by the leading of the Holy Spirit. He has faith that the Spirit has already evaluated his circumstances, and he trusts what the Spirit says.

The reality of God can be experienced only in moment-by-moment faith. A moment-by-moment relationship with the Holy Spirit is possible when you believe God is in control; believe that everything that happens is either caused by or allowed by God; and believe that God always wants what's best for you.

Rather than responding to the darts of life with your limited knowledge of good and evil, respond to them with the Tree of Life, the living Jesus Christ. Trust that as you turn to the Holy Spirit in every situation, He will give you what you need.

Part Four

Understanding
Your Choice

Holy Spirit High School

If you want to walk in the Spirit, you'll need to attend Holy Spirit High School daily. The tests can be hard, but the Instructor is wonderful. And you'll especially enjoy the graduation party!

Salvation is not some dusty doctrine in theological textbooks. It is a reality that can be experienced right at the point of contact when a problem hits.

In Holy Spirit High School you will study all the lessons of life. You'll learn about pride, arrogance, hate, fear, lust, selfishness, covetousness, and more -- and discover how to deal correctly with them, with the leading of the Holy Spirit, at the moment they strike.

"Normal" self-led Christians go for days without really asking the Holy Spirit for help. They deal with the darts of life with their limited knowledge of good and evil. They don't understand that there is a new and better way, and they continue to walk in the strength of their flesh.

They may go for days not speaking to the Holy Spirit, until the number of darts sticking into them causes them to cry out to

God for deliverance. Many Christians go from church service to church service barely able to make it to the next "fill-up."

Why wait until you're incapacitated before you turn to God? The new way, provided by Jesus, is that you turn to the Holy Spirit within you at the moment a difficulty hits you. At that very moment, He will show you the way to deal with it so that it will disappear.

There are two good reasons for this:

1) You won't carry around darts that erode your faith and relationship with Jesus. As long as you carry a problem or temptation in your soul, you are to some extent incapacitated. The devil has one less warrior to fight.

2) You'll learn of the Holy Spirit moment by moment. You'll experience His salvation in action, right on the battleground of life. Dealing with the dart at the point of contact enables you to look at it closely and learn about it. Perhaps you will see how the dart is constructed, and the Holy Spirit can show you how to deal with it before it strikes again.

What's A Dart?

A dart is anything that takes away your peace, joy, and love in the Holy Spirit. A dart can come from your own subconscious mind and heart, from something that is said or that happens to you, or it can come directly from the enemy.

Darts take your attention away from God's peace, joy and love, and focus it on something unpleasant.

Darts undermine your faith in God. The reason a dart feels bad is that it causes you to doubt that God loves you and is in control of your life. When you gave yourself completely to God, you were set free of the pain of self, and received God's Life in its place. But when a dart hits, it revives the old pain.

A dart causes your soul to doubt God. You suspect that He has broken His promise to be your all in all, because He has allowed adversity. It seems your Savior is not as wonderful as you had hoped, and you're back where you started. This is similar to the ploy that snagged Adam and Eve. It can be overcome only by faith.

Deep within all of us there is a desire to be loved completely. We desire completeness in God, with no pain to "ruin" our relationship. The reason why this desire is so real in us is that God put it there.

Everyone tries to fulfill the desire for unending love. Some do it by searching for satisfaction in drugs, immoral relationships and other perversions.

The desire for complete and utter fulfillment in God's love is the Blessed Hope. To some extent we can experience it today, but it will become a full reality when we go to heaven to be with Him. In the meantime, we still crave that love. And when we give our everything to Jesus, we expect Him to give His all to us -- which we think means preventing bad things from happening to us.

So when something bad does happen to us, our soul (mind and heart), the enemy, and the world tell us our trust in Him was in vain. This is a jolt to our faith. We doubt that He loves us unconditionally, that He's really in control. This is the root of the pain we feel when a dart hits.

To paraphrase Psalm 50, it would be easy to deal with betrayal if it came from an enemy, but you can't bear the thought that it came from a friend with whom you have made a covenant (promise). The hurt caused by the dart penetrates deeper than the dart itself. The hurt is that God allowed it.

The questions of whether He really loves you or not, and whether He really is in control, are both foundational faith issues. They are the two pillars on which your entire relationship with God rests.

The answer, of course, is that God allows the darts for your own good. More specifically, God allows the darts so that your faith will grow in Him, which is the definition of Good for you. If you do not have this faith, you will seek peace, but like waves driven and tossed by the wind (Isaiah 57:20), you will not find it.

Self-inflicted darts

Many of the darts that pierce you come from within. These are thoughts and feelings that have no place in the heart and mind of a Spirit-led Christian.

God allows you to continue to shoot darts at yourself so that you will finally turn to Him in faith and say, "I've had enough of this pain. I'm not going to think about this garbage anymore. Jesus, you died so that I'd be free of myself. It was crucified on the cross with you. Please take this away from me and help me to confess continually your victory in my life."

Enemy-inflicted darts

Many of the darts thrown by the enemy are vain imaginations. Most have no substance in themselves; they merely give a perception of a real or imagined situation. Dealing with this type of dart is simple: Don't believe it. Treat it the same as a self- inflicted dart.

God allows these darts to hit you so that you will turn to Jesus and say, "I know you died on the cross so I wouldn't have to worry about the future. I know that this is not the Holy Spirit talking, but rather the father of lies. I renounce these thoughts and feelings and I command Satan to leave me alone, in the name of Jesus Christ."

Life-inflicted darts

These are a key issue for the Spirit-led Christian. Whether the darts of life come from the enemy or from circumstances that seem like coincidence, God allows them to happen to you.

Many Spirit-led Christians can stand in faith in their spirits and souls without difficulty. They can tell the devil he's a liar. They can tell their minds and hearts that they are liars. They can tell the Holy Spirit that everything is wonderful. They can speak forth God's love and lordship over every aspect of their lives...until disaster strikes.

It is significant that psychiatry and modern Christianity prefer to deal more with self-inflicted and Satan-inflicted darts rather than those that are life-inflicted. This issue can divide congregations. Few people are willing to take the biblical stand that everything that happens to born-again Christians is either caused by or allowed by God.

The reason for living is to love God with all that is in you. If you do this, you'll have to lose your self and many things that are dear to you. Forsaking self and those things you desire outside of God are what darts are all about. Darts reveal where your heart is. They pinpoint desires outside of God.

Darts are like germs that attack a physical body. Most do no harm. But occasionally, a germ will find no antibody to fight it. In the Spirit-led Christian, occasionally a dart will find no faith to fight it. The dart reveals that your faith in God needs to increase in a certain area.

God can heal your illness. God can change your desperate situation. God can bring all types of victory to your life. As you look to Him in faith, He can change your life. But He must be your reason for living, not what He can do for you.

So many want the power of God, but not the Person of God. Get to know Him, and desire His will for your life more than your will for your life. Look at His face, not just at His hands. Trust that he has a bigger plan for your life than you may realize.

God wants the whole body to grow up in Him

When you give your life to Jesus, you agree to follow Him, whatever His game plan. This may involve suffering for the sake of the body of Christ and for the lost. The apostle Paul, for example, suffered many times for the good of the body of Christ.

As you grow in Jesus, God may allow darts to hit you for the sake of someone else. If you deal with a dart correctly in the Holy Spirit, it may be for the sake of another Christian, or to help bring someone into the Kingdom. You might be thrown into prison unjustly, as Paul was, so that you can witness to a particular prisoner. The challenge of enduring an unpleasant situation may do more than help you grow in God, it may allow you to help someone else grow in God.

Whatever the source of the dart, it should be dealt with correctly in the Holy Spirit. Whether it is for your own benefit or for the benefit of another, use it to increase your faith.

How To Deal With A Dart

God designed you to feel pain when the health of your body is threatened. When a thorn pricks your skin, you know you need to remove it to make the pain stop. It is the same with your soul. When a dart pierces your soul, you feel bad and want to relieve the pain.

Unfortunately, many of us have become so used to our souls hurting that we think it's a necessary thing. As the song goes, "Suffering is the only thing that made me feel alive. That's just how much it costs to survive in this world."

So when a dart has pierced your soul, making you feel guilt, sadness, uneasiness or worry, you may live with it and assume it's a part of you. Don't be deceived. Jesus paid the price for your sin. You needn't hold onto those bad feelings any longer. Remove the dart by cooperating with the Holy Spirit.

Turn to the Holy Spirit and He will show you how deal with the dart. For example, if a dart reminds you that you have a physical flaw, the Holy Spirit may in turn remind you that you are beautiful to Jesus, and that's what really matters. If a dart says, "You'll be poor all your life," the Holy Spirit may remind you that you are rich in Jesus. He may tell you to be anxious for nothing (Philippians 4:6), and to be content that Jesus will supply your every need.

When A Dart Hits A Self-led Christian

1) He begins his day with his mind at peace.

2) ZAP! A dart hits: He remembers that a certain man insulted him, saying that Christians are a bunch of hypocrites. He feels the attack personally.

3) The dart hurts, and he wants it removed. He pulls it out the only way he knows how, with his knowledge of good and evil (which may include biblical truth). He can only pull out the part of the dart he can see.

4) He goes on with part of the dart still sticking in him, which causes him to lose peace and intimacy with God. He has yet to realize that only the Holy Spirit can help him deal with the remaining bad feelings caused by the insult.

When A Dart Hits A Self-led Christian

5) Later that day, he receives and deals with more darts.

6) Still later, he is so anxious, discouraged and distracted that he is unable to remove even the parts of the darts he can see.

7) Finally, he can no longer carry on. He looks to God and asks Him to take away the darts and make him new. (See next section for details on how to do this.)

8) He continues his day with his mind at peace.

When A Dart Hits A Spirit-led Christian

1) His thoughts are full of praise and thanksgiving for God's peace, joy and love.

2) ZAP! The dart hits. He remembers that a man insulted him, and he feels resentful.

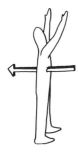

3) The dart is painful; he wants it removed, so he turns to the Holy Spirit within his spirit. He is led to forgive the man. He then asks God to forgive him, as well, for the hard feelings he had toward the man. He then prays for him with the love of God.

4) He resumes occupying his mind with confessions of God's goodness.

When A Dart Hits A Spirit-led Christian

5) Zap! Another dart hits, threatening his inner peace and intimacy with Jesus.

6) He turns to the Holy Spirit within him and asks how to deal with the dart. He follows the Spirit's advice and the dart is gone.

7) He resumes his intimate awareness of God, continuing to focus on Him regardless of circumstances.

8) Darts continue to hit him, but he deals with each one immediately, according to the leading of the Spirit.

A Day In The Life
Of A Spirit-led Christian

How you deal with each dart represents a defeat or a victory in your walk in the Spirit. To illustrate this, let's follow a Spirit-led Christian through a typical day -- one filled with routine events that seem inconsequential, yet make a significant impact on his peace of mind and overall happiness.

He gets up early to go to work while his spouse sleeps in. As he quietly brushes his teeth, a thought comes to his mind: He gets up early for other people, why can't they get up with him? He is unsure of the origin of this thought, but trusts it is a good one -- after all, the Bible says to bear one another's burdens. He is unaware that the thought is a dart designed to undermine his relationship with the Holy Spirit.

The way he deals with this dart will set the tone for the day. If he listens to his soul (heart and mind), he will have a dart sticking in him that will make him unable to see clearly. As more darts hit him during the day, they will make it harder for him to hear the still, small voice of the Holy Spirit. The more pain he feels in his soul, the harder it will be for him to discern the Spirit's gentle voice.

He remembers he is supposed to continually confess that Jesus is Lord and thank Him and praise Him for all He is to him. Yet after he has worshipped Jesus for a while, the thought of asking his spouse to get out of bed returns.

His heart and mind say, "Nobody appreciates me. I have to get up by myself and suffer so they can lounge around. It's not fair. They're taking advantage of me. I should wake everybody up and tell them how I feel."

Fortunately, he turns to the Holy Spirit within his spirit and he discerns the truth: "You are not your own, you are bought with a price (1 Corinthians 6:19-20). You do not need others to appreciate you in order to feel good about yourself. I love you and gave My life for you. Do not be self-aware. Worship Me and I will give you My peace and joy and love."

He silently walks out of the bedroom and is told by his spirit, "Go back and give your spouse a kiss and tell her you love her."

He's almost out the door and his spirit says, "Go, do the same with your children."

Now he is running for the bus and just misses it. The thought comes to his mind, "If I hadn't spent time with my family I wouldn't have risked being late to work. God blew it. He didn't protect me from failing."

The Christian is momentarily confused, for he thinks he is listening to his soul tell him the "truth." He wonders if he is deceiving himself. It is at this point his faith will grow or diminish. How a Christian deals with something he perceives as bad determines his progress in his walk with the Holy Spirit.

Consider: Who says that missing a bus is bad? Who determines what is good or bad in a Christian's life? Is it the

Christian, working with a limited knowledge of good and evil --
and with a limited mental capacity? Is it the Christian himself,
who can't see beyond a limited perspective? God, after all, is the
only One who knows endings as well as beginnings, the only One
who has all problems solved before they happen.

When a Christian is Spirit-led, he can access infinite
knowledge. God doesn't make decisions based on limited
information. He does what He does and allows what He allows
because of unlimited understanding. When you partake of the
knowledge of the Holy Spirit, you tap into the definition of logic
itself. God IS. That says it all. He doesn't merely have
intelligence, He IS intelligence. God doesn't simply possess
knowledge, He IS knowledge.

But let's return to the Spirit-led Christian, who has just
missed his bus. He now has a choice: He can assume that God
made a mistake, he didn't hear God correctly, or he imagined
God told him to take time to be loving toward his family. Or he
can stand in faith: Regardless of why he missed the bus, God
allowed it, and God always wants what's best for him.

So he turns to the Holy Spirit within his spirit and says, "I
know things don't just happen by coincidence, and I know that
You have a plan in all this. Please help me to not worry about the
future. Please take care of things at my job so I don't get in
trouble, unless that is your will for some reason I don't
understand. Thank you, Jesus."

With that act of faith in Jesus as his Saviour and Lord, he
just removed the dart. The poison of the dart will do no damage
to his faith nor to his relationship with the Holy Spirit. He can
resume his continual confession of God's goodness.

Because he again is open to the Holy Spirit's leading, he is
receptive to being used by the Spirit when a neighbor sits next to
him. He hears his spirit when it says, "Ask him why he looks so
depressed." The Holy Spirit then gives him words of sympathy
and compassion that help his neighbor and also glorify God. He
speaks words of life that God may use to help the neighbor to be

set free of self and to accept Jesus as his Saviour and Lord.

As he rides the bus, the Spirit-led Christian is continually aware of how wonderful Jesus is and thanks Him for using him in a precious way. He knows that if he had not dealt correctly with the dart of missing the bus, he would not have been able to hear the Holy Spirit's voice concerning the neighbor. Now he is ready for -- even expecting -- the Holy Spirit to use him throughout the day as a source of light to illuminate others' lives.

He arrives at work and punches the time clock seconds before his starting time. He thanks and praises Jesus for getting him to work on time. He also praises Him for saving him from worrying on the way so that he could enjoy His presence and talk with the neighbor.

He goes to his work station, filled with peace and praise, and starts a project. Then a fellow employee says, "The job you did yesterday was rejected by the customer. Do it over."

The soul (heart and mind) of the Christian feels resentment and responds silently to the other worker, "You're not my boss. Who are you to tell me to do the job over? Besides, the customer was wrong to reject my work -- it was perfect."

But he turns to the Holy Spirit within his spirit and receives very different advice: "Forgive the fellow employee for talking like he's your boss. Ask God to forgive you and to remove your resentment. Tell your fellow employee you'll take care of the problem as soon as possible. Then pray for him."

The boss comes in and tells the Spirit-led Christian what a mess he has made of things. The customer is mad and wants his money back.

The Christian's soul speaks within him, "I did a good job. That customer is wrong. Did my fellow employee have anything to do with this? I'll bet the customer was told the job wasn't good so that I'd get into trouble."

But he immediately turns to the Holy Spirit within his spirit, and he hears, "Tell the boss you're sorry for any trouble you've caused. Explain that you thought the job was done correctly, but you'll be happy to make it right with the customer. Forgive your boss for being unkind to you and pray for him."

A thought comes to the Christian's mind: "That other employee is trying to turn the boss against me. I had better defend myself to the boss and tell him how the fellow is taking extra breaks and not working hard."

The Christian doesn't know where this thought came from. It may be his own soul trying to protect its pride and self-image, or it might be a dart from the enemy. But it doesn't matter where the dart came from, there is just one way for a Spirit-led Christian to deal with it.

He communes with the Holy Spirit within his spirit and he hears, "You forgave the fellow employee for his bad attitude, over an hour ago. Continue to forgive him and pray for his salvation. You know that God won't let your boss do anything to you outside of His will. If He allows your boss to fire you, that's God's concern. Remember you are really working for Him. If you're supposed to defend yourself to your boss, God will give you a peace about that. In the meantime, pray for your boss."

Later he brushes against a table where someone left a pail of nails. Hundreds of nails fall and scatter over the floor.

His first reaction is anger. His soul says, "Who is the idiot that left those nails on the table? I'm not going to clean them up. I've got too much work to do today already without this. I'll bet my fellow employee left it there. I should give him a piece of my mind."

But then he turns to the Holy Spirit within his spirit and knows, "Jesus loves you. You are His joy. You do things for Him, not for man. Be a good example and show the love of Jesus. Pick up the nails and say, 'I love you Jesus,' as you pick them up. Let every nail be a symbol of your love for Him. Pray for your fellow employee."

Throughout the day he deals with darts according to the

leading of the Holy Spirit. And when he is not dealing with darts, he is confessing continually that Jesus is his Saviour and Lord. This keeps the darts down to a minimum. And this is the importance of continual confession; without it, a Christian's worldly mind and heart will try to tear him down.

Your soul will try and persuade you to return to it for guidance. As a Spirit-led Christian, you know that your soul contains the old man that Jesus saved you from. Rather than listening to your world-led heart and mind, follow the leading of the Holy Spirit.

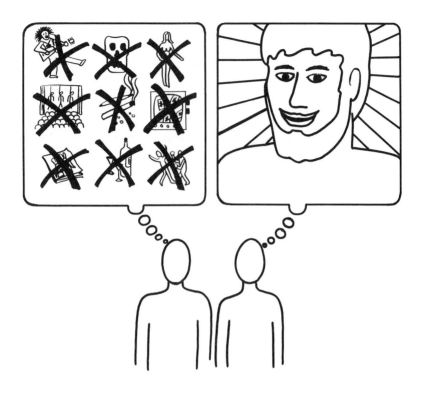

Overcoming Sin

You cannot overcome sin simply by applying rules and laws to your life. If you try to live that way, you will be a self-led Christian, not a Spirit-led Christian.

The Spirit-led Christian doesn't try to fight sin. Rather, he turns to the Creator of the universe and contemplates Him, and the temptation evaporates.

The self-led Christian uses his mind to remember rules and laws in order to keep himself from sinning.

For example, when he sees a pornographic magazine in a convenience store, he may shut his mind to prevent it from receiving information. He stops any thought of sex and keeps pushing the thought out of his mind. In the process of trying to stop these thoughts, he may close an entire room in his mind that has to do with sexual pleasure.

Instead of walking out of the convenience store with a whole mind, he has shut down an entire room so that there's no chance of having any thoughts of sexual pleasure. And this is not the will of God in his life.

The Spirit gives life

But what happens if a Spirit-led Christian walks in and sees the same magazine? Since he is dwelling on Jesus, and having an ongoing communication with Him, he barely notices it. But if seeing it is unavoidable, he may respond to it. He immediately turns to Jesus and says, "I'm sorry, I shouldn't have these feelings for women other than my wife. Please forgive me." And he continues his confessing that Jesus is his Lord.

If the unwelcome thoughts return, he may say, "Jesus, Please help me to think only of my wife that way," and he continues confessing that Jesus is his Lord.

If the thoughts return later on, he may say, "Jesus, please help those who are responsible for the magazine to be saved, and help me not to think of it again. Thank you Jesus." And he continues confessing that Jesus is his Lord. "Jesus you're wonderful. You give me all I need. You're my heart's desire. Thank you Jesus."

Rather than spending effort to fight sin, the Spirit-led Christian dwells on God, and receives His Life. This is the way sin is overcome.

Part five

Understanding
Your Life

The House You Live In

Your soul can be viewed as a house with many different rooms. The house should have all its doors unlocked, so that all rooms are accessible to the Holy Spirit.

Self-led Christians lock the doors of the rooms of their minds with rules and laws. They don't understand that God wants them to walk in the power of the Holy Spirit. With His help, Christians can look at sin truthfully, and fearlessly.

Some people refuse the help of the Holy Spirit, and choose to close off certain rooms of their minds. As we saw in the previous chapter, this occasionally is done with rooms that have to do with sexual desire.

It's true that Jesus said that if a part of you causes you to sin, to cut it off (Matthew 5:29-30). This stresses the seriousness of sin and the importance of dealing with it. He also said that anyone who looks at a woman lustfully has already committed adultery with her in his heart (Matthew 5:28). This stresses the importance of having a clean thought-life.

But when Christians try to put an end to lustful thoughts by shutting down the rooms of their minds that have to do with sexual desire, they make it impossible to help others who have sexual problems. When they see someone caught in a sexual sin, such as adultery, homosexuality or prostitution, they are likely to have feelings of revulsion. That room is closed and they are unable to view sex -- and sinners -- the way the Holy Spirit wants them to.

Allow the Holy Spirit to throw open the doors of fear, disgust and guilt. Allow God to examine everything in the room, and to tell you how to think about those things. Allow Him to renew your mind.

He wants you to be able to look at the contents of the rooms in the light of His presence. He wants a Christian to understand, for example, that sexual pleasure is godly in the context of marriage. He wants him to see that those who commit sexual sins have the same sexual desire that he does, but it has been terribly twisted.

The Spirit-led Christian needn't fear being defiled. The Holy Spirit isn't afraid of defilement. He is in you so that you can know the truth, and so that the truth will make you free (John 8:32). That freedom is not so you can sin, but so you can experience life. God's Life will enable you to deal with sinners on their level, to express the love of God without judgement or condescension. It enables you to understand them, and love them, as God does.

You will look past their outward appearance and their sinful actions and see the person that God created and wants to redeem.

Other rooms

There are other rooms in a Christian's house that may be inaccessible to the Holy Spirit. For example, many Christians close the room that has to do with giving money.

Since they don't trust God to supply their every need, they can't give money easily. After the fifth beggar asks them for spare change, they close the room that has to do with loving strangers. And maybe that room is connected to one that has to do with loving their in-laws, so they close that room, too.

Perhaps they have closed the room that has to do with sharing about God. Perhaps they've been rejected by friends when telling them about Jesus. So now, when they have a perfect opportunity to tell someone how much Jesus means to them, they just stand there and say nothing. The words are locked up in that room.

Maybe you, like many other Christians, have only a few rooms you leave open. And perhaps it has been this way so long you can't even remember why some of the rooms are closed. You are used to living in two or three rooms.

After all, in some ways it's easier to live in just two or three rooms. It's easier to keep just a few rooms tidy. If you're walking in the strength of your own self, then it's wearying to have to keep a lot of rooms clean. It's far easier to just close off several rooms.

One of the beauties of the Spirit-led life is that the Holy Spirit lets you know when a room needs to be cleaned. So even if you have all the rooms in the house open, the only one you need to be concerned with is the particular room the Holy Spirit directs you to deal with.

He continually walks through the rooms of your mind. As He passes through, His gentle breeze freshens them. He shows you how to open the windows and draw the curtains, and to let God's love fill every corner.

No secret room

Finally, there is no need for a "secret" room, the room where many Christians go in order to sin. That room also can be opened and made ready for the in-dwelling Holy Spirit.

When all the rooms are opened, and a person becomes a balanced, healthy, Spirit-led Christian, he will have no desire to hide from the Holy Spirit. And when he is able to show all the rooms of his house, he can be confident, with the leading of the Holy Spirit, that his house will not be defiled.

You can be an effective tool in the hands of the Holy Spirit, and be used by Him to set others free. With all rooms of your mind open to the Holy Spirit, you can understand, and be exposed to, the sin of other people -- and not be affected by it.

The Holy Spirit wants to renew your mind. He wants to transform you from glory to glory. But he can't do that if you've locked Him out.

"Behold, I stand at the door and knock; if anyone hears My voice and opens the door, I will come in to him, and will dine with him, and he with Me." (Revelation 3:20)

How To View Yourself

The **self-led** Christian sees himself as OK when his good deeds at least balance out his bad deeds. He may not get home for dinner on time, but at least he brought flowers for his wife. The way he deals with guilt is by doing good deeds. Only then does he sense God's approval, and feel "worthy" of God's love.

His idea of God's attitude toward him is based on how he feels. If he feels guilty, he assumes God is angry. If he is proud of his good deeds, he feels God is pleased with him.

The **Spirit-led** Christian sees himself as useless in himself, unable to do good deeds on his own. He realizes that only when the Holy Spirit leads him in a good deed does it become "good." His strength is knowing God loves him no matter how bad things get.

As God's peace, joy, and love pour on him moment by moment, he submits himself to the Holy Spirit in all things.

His good feelings are based on who God is and what He has done. The Spirit-led Christian walks by faith in God, not by faith in himself.

How To Look At Life

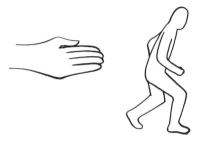 

The self-led Christian lacks a correct concept of where he is in relationship to God. He functions by his own knowledge of good and evil. He sees only what exists in the self-contained box of his soul.

He considers himself free. He thinks God has given him the tools for living his life, and now it is his responsibility to do the best he can with them.

His joy is in his dreams, delusions, self-fulfillment and desires. He is motivated by fear and insecurity. His peace, joy, and love are circumstantial; they come and go as the circumstances of his life change.

The Spirit-led Christian walks by faith in who God is, and by what God wants. He has crucified his "self" and looks to God for everything he needs.

He has God's peace, joy, love -- and God's manifested presence. He is secure in Jesus, and is not motivated by fear.

His walking realities are those promises made to him in the Bible: that God will take care of him and love him, and that he will someday experience the Blessed Hope.

How To Keep Clean

The **self-led** Christian recognizes sin and knows how to ask for God's forgiveness. But there's another kind of uncleanliness he's only vaguely aware of: fears and doubts that stem from a lack of faith in God. He may not see these fears and doubts as sin, but they affect him just the same -- and they can make him so uncomfortable he will become more worldly.

Self-led Christians who feel distant from God tend to wash themselves with religious acts. These make them feel clean for a while, but also lead to hypocrisy.

The **Spirit-led** Christian cares about nothing except the will of God. He knows his life is in God's hands, so he rarely experiences fear or doubt. But when he does, it is only for a moment; he then turns to the Holy Spirit and those negative feelings are dealt with correctly.

When he turns to the Holy Spirit, he is washed with living water. This cleansing is an ongoing process initiated by the Spirit-led Christian. Like the apostle Peter, the Spirit-led Christian says to Jesus, "cleanse me" throughout his day.

How To Give To Others

The self-led Christian is afraid to give money away because he's not sure God will take care of him financially. He is afraid he'll be without money in the future. He mistrusts God and suspects God wants him to part with his money so that he'll suffer. He doubts that God will look out for him, so he keeps his money in order to look out for himself.

The Spirit-led Christian isn't afraid to part with his money when the Holy Spirit tells him to. He knows that God's love is his only treasure. He also knows that all he has comes from God and belongs to God. If the Holy Spirit says, "Give," then as a steward, he gives, and enjoys seeing people blessed by it.

Idols In Your Life

Idols are anything in your life you think you need but really don't. Idols are whatever receives your time, talents and affections to the exclusion of God.

Idols can be things that seem godly, and they may appear to have the best religious reasons behind them. Your idols may even define the way you see yourself. And because they may be part of your identity, they can be very hard to recognize. Only the Holy Spirit can show you the truth about them. Ask Him to reveal your idols to you as you study the scriptures.

Christians who are truly submitted to God give up their idols as soon as they recognize them. It is more painful for Christians who resist, because they go through a process of wrestling with the knowledge of the Holy Spirit.

When this is happening, a Christian tends to avoid the Holy Spirit, since His presence reminds him of what He has asked him to do. But eventually the Christian will grow tired of fighting what he knows is right, and he will come to desire the peace of the Holy Spirit instead of the idol. As he grows in the Spirit, he will learn to relinquish other idols as soon as he recognizes them.

Freedom means having nothing to lose. As you give up your idols, you gain freedom. This is what the exchanged life of the born-again Christian is all about: You lose your self and gain Him.

When you give up your idols, you'll see them as valueless compared to the living God. Lavish your time and affections on Him; He is the eternal joy of all who worship Him.

The Blessed Hope

The early Christians understood something so fantastic they spoke of it often. There are numerous references to it in the New Testament, and it is a primary fact of the Christian outlook.

To dwell on the Blessed Hope is to dwell on Jesus, for He IS the Blessed Hope. His will is that someday you will be with Him in paradise. He looks forward to that day, and so should you. That is when your relationship with Him will be consummated.

Christians today hear about this frequently, and may think they understand it, but their knowledge is superficial. Yet for the early Christians, the Blessed Hope was a living, burning reality that consumed their every thought and deed.

Many early Christians endured terrible hardships because they refused to deny Jesus. For example, when given the chance to avoid torture or death by throwing incense on the altar of a false god, they refused to do it.

They knew that even if they gained the whole world, it wasn't worth losing their souls.

And they knew that after their physical bodies were destroyed, paradise awaited them.

Let us not be so sophisticated we can't enjoy pleasurable thoughts of the fantastic future that awaits us. For no other reason, this alone should lift our spirits to untouchable heights.

When we focus our awareness on how it will be when we are fully with Jesus -- in the absence of sin, fear, hate and pain -- nothing that comes our way can bring us down. This sustained the early Christians, and it can sustain us today.

"Beloved, now we are the children of God, and it has not appeared as yet what we shall be. We know that, when He appears, we shall be like Him, because we shall see Him just as He is. And everyone who has this hope fixed on Him purifies himself, just as He is pure." (1 John 3:2-3)

As they become available, **additional publications, including teaching materials based on Intimacy With God will be announced** to those on our mailing list.

To be placed on the mailing list, or to contact the author, write White Harvest Publishing, P.O. Box 97, Mammoth Spring, AR 72554.

To order books directly from the publisher, write for an order form or call 1-800-598-0584.

Quantity discounts are available to evangelistic organizations.

About the author:

Patrick McIntyre, author of <u>Intimacy With God</u>, currently makes his home in a small town in Arkansas where he serves as youth pastor of his church. During the last 20 years he has worked in evangelism in the United States and Mexico.

If you are not sure what it means to be born again, this page is for you.

The Bible says all of us are dirty with sin. If we want to be intimate with God, we must first be washed clean. but if we try to do this by being good, we will fail. We can never be good enough to stand in the presence of a perfect God. Only God Himself can wash our sins away--*supernaturally*.

This is the reason for the cross of Jesus Christ. God is just, and requires a just punishment for your sins. You deserve death, but God wants to give you life. So He took the punishment you deserve. He suffered the pain for all your sins, and He died physically so that you can live spiritually.

The way is open for you to know God intimately, moment by moment, as Adam and Eve once did. You must first receive the sacrifice Jesus made for you and ask Him to come into your spirit. He wants to save you from the just punishment you deserve. You must yield your life to Him completely.

Here are some words you can say to Him:

Dear Lord Jesus,

I Know I am a sinner and need Your forgiveness.

I know You died for me. Please forgive my sins. I want to stop sinning.

I now ask You to come into me, to save me from my sins now, and forever more.

I give you everything I am and ask You to take over my life and make me new.

I want to trust You as my Saviour and follow You as the only Lord of my life.

Thank you Jesus.

These words are a vow. When you say them, and really mean them in your deepest being, Jesus will come into your spirit by the power of the Holy Spirit.

You are now what the Bible calls, "born again." You now have God in you. You have a new spirit because He is there. This is the beginning of a NEW LIFE for you.

You now need to be with others who belong to Him. Ask Jesus to direct you to a group of Christians who believe the Bible is 100% true. Also, ask Jesus to give you a desire to read His words -- the Bible. A good place to start is the Gospel of John (The 4th book in the New Testament). In the third chapter of John is Jesus' own explanation of what it means to be born again.

If you have questions, you are welcome to contact the author of this book.